Doctor Dwarf

AND OTHER POEMS FOR CHILDREN BY
A.M. KLEIN

ILLUSTRATED BY

Gail Geltner

EDITED BY

Mary Alice Downie
and
Barbara Robertson

Quarry Press

In memory of A.M. Klein

Song To Be Sung at Dawn

Heigh ho! the rooster crows!
The rooster crows upon the thatch;
A dog leaps up to pull at a latch;
The dew is on the rose.
The daisies open: they shine like money;
The bees are busy gathering honey;
The pigeons hop on their toes.
The birds chirp underneath the eaves;
They sing from their nests among the leaves;
The sun is in the skies!
The barn is bright; the meadow sunny;
The sun smiles into every cranny.
A little boy rubs his eyes, —
A little boy rubs his eyes and nose,
And says his *Modeh Ani.*

Jonah

Within the whale's belly
Good Jonah at home
Ate fish made of jelly
And drank frothy foam.

O, all the whale swallowed
Stood him in good stead,
From coral he hollowed
A table and bed.

The lobsters which wandered
Beneath the whale's nose
Beheld pincers sundered
To hang Jonah's clothes.

A mermaiden chatted
With Jonah, who found
Her rushes she matted
For slippery ground.

On the heart of the whale, he
Carefully stuck
The round leaf of lily
And made him a clock.

O Jonah, the wizard,
O Jonah, the free'd,
Did drape the whale's gizzard
With fragrant seaweed.

A pearl from an oyster
Brought light out of shade.
O how they did roister,
Did Jonah and maid!

Until the Lord wished him
Back to his host,
And whale-gullet dished him
Upon a rough coast.

Heaven at Last

I have seen a lark
Swallow a worm, soar, and disappear
In a blue oblivion.
Wherefore I consoled myself, saying:
It is not too terrible to die
To be eaten by worms,
Provided
Considerate skylarks bear the worms aloft
And lay them at the Upper Gates . . .

Counting-Out Rhyme

Orange, citron, fig and date,
While the fruit buds, we stand and wait;
Flower on branch, and grape on vine,
One of us soon will leave the line.
Blossoms burst, the fruit will swell,
Who it will be, one can not tell.
Almond, raisin, olive, plum.
The word is hush, the sign is mum.
Oh, the sun shone, Oh, the wind blew,
The apple fell to this little Jew.

Market Song

Plump pigeons, who will buy?
Plump pigeons, and fat doves?
Come, gossips, hurry nigh;
Shake purses, hearty loves,
    And buy my doves.

Oh, cheap at any price,
A most delicious morsel,
Made ready in a trice!
Take home a feathered parcel,
    A dainty morsel.

Wives, do you love your men?
Set love upon a plate.
A good bird is worth ten
Grown bony in a crate.
    Wives, do not wait!

Go feel them, look at them —
Their breasts, their bright pink eyes!
You buy the like of them
Elsewhere, and at my price,
  My petty price?

Unknot your kerchiefs, then,
Shake out your coins, my loves, —
Buy now, you know not when
You will catch such fat doves,
  Such doves again.

Elijah

Elijah in a long beard
With a little staff
Hobbles through the market
And makes the children laugh.

He crows like a rooster,
He dances like a bear,
While the long-faced rabbis
Drop their jaws to stare.

He tosses his skullcap
To urchin and tot,
And catches it neatly
Right on his bald spot.

And he can tell stories
Of lovers who elope;
And terrible adventures
With cardinal and pope.

Without a single pinch, and
Without a blow or cuff,
We learned from him the Aleph,
We learned from him the Tauph.

Between the benedictions
We would play leapfrog —
O, this was a wonderful
Synagogue!

He can make a whistle
From a gander's quill;
He can make a mountain
Out of a molehill.

Oh, he is a great man!
Wished he, he could whoop
The moon down from heaven,
And roll it like a hoop;

Wished he, he could gather
The stars from the skies,
And juggle them like marbles
Before our very eyes.

Wandering Beggar

Who envies not this beggar, who
Sits in the sunny market place,
Shaking the pebbles from his shoe,
Knotting again his torn shoe-lace?

From daisied path, from dusty road,
From cobbled ways, and country lanes
Hither he hops from his abode
In gypsy wagons and huckster wains.

Come, children of the town, and hear
What tales this jolly traveller brings,
What coloured tiding he doth bear,
What foreign-sounding songs he sings.

Though it be true that in his purse
A small green penny sleeps alone,
And in his sack, two crusty loaves,
One mouldy, and one hard as stone, —

Consider but the towns he saw,
The curious hamlets, the queer inns!
The road his realm, a song his law
And he an incognito prince!

Who wants for burgher's clothes? Do not
This beggar's tatters sweetly smell
Of sleeping in a grassy spot,
Of lazing in a fragrant dell?

And what the sight of gold coin to
One who has lately gazed upon
The kingdom of the small red Jew,
The turbulent Sambation?

Doctor Dwarf

Into his beard he laughs at the
Musty apothecaries;
A doctor, and no quack is he,
He learns his lore from fairies.

And if there is an ill for which
He knows no herb himself,
He goes not to the broomstick witch,
He hies him to the elf.

Is there a little boy who's ill?
A little lad who's hurt?
He gives him an almond for a pill,
A raisin for dessert.

He takes the blindman from his hut
To see the moon i' the sky.
'A ladder!' the blind man cries, 'to cut
Two slices of that pie!'

A lover pined away for love,
He could not dine nor sup;
Until the wise man poured for him
Dew from a buttercup.

There was a hunchback in our town,
He was so hunched, was he,
That when he looked up he still looked down.
Now he's as straight as me.

With a pine needle and some hay
He sewed my cousin's stitches;
Oh, it was such a sunny day
When he broke my brother's crutches!

He lived on the hill; and in his time
One never moaned in pain
For longer than it takes to climb
The hill, and down again.

King Elimelech

King Elimelech —
A dent in his crown,
A twist in his sceptre —
Limps through the town.

He hawks little trinkets,
He cries his small wares;
He gets him a table
At all the town fairs.

'Ho, goodman, will you buy
A patched purple robe,
Aristocrat garters,
My last wizard's globe?

'Farthings buy medals;
A penny will buy
My most potent signet,
My bright heraldry.

'Yea, I will barter
This throne from whence I rule
For a much more cosy
Artisan's stool.'

The pedigreed peddler
Flaunts his strange goods,
But yokel and bumpkin
Chaffer for foods.

Such gauds are costly —
The peasant folk say —
With straws and pebbles
Let children play.

Alas, these are hard times,
When even a crowned head
Can not get his daily
Butter and bread.

If kings will not hunger
Then let them all fast!
So said King Eli-
Melech the Last.

Junk-Dealer

All week his figure mottles
   The city lanes,
Hawking his rags and bottles
   In quaint refrains.

But on the High, the Holy
   Days, he is lord;
And being lord, earth wholly,
   Gladly is abhorred.

While litanies are clamored,
   His loud voice brags
A Hebrew most ungrammared.
   He sells God rags.

Rev Owl

Erudite, solemn,
The pious bird
Sits on a tree,
His *shtreimel* furred.

The owl, chief rabbi
Of the woods,
In moonlight ponders
Worldly goods.

With many a legal
To who? To wit?
He nightly parses
Holy writ.

And then tears gizzards
Of captured fowl
To find them kosher
For an owl.

A *Psalm of a Mighty Hunter before the Lord*

O, not for furs,
And not for feathers,
Did Chatzkel the hunter
Weather all weathers!

Neither the crow,
Nor the shy sparrow
Had fear of his bow
And rotted arrow.

A hunter he was,
Who bore no rifle
Whose snare did not kill,
Nor lariat stifle.

A dearth in the land:
Beasts die of famine —
Chatzkel the hunter
Leaves his backgammon

Traps him some wild beasts,
Keeps them in cages,
Until the hot sun will
Have spent its rages.

Meanwhile the tiger
Eats tiger-lilies,
And milk is fed to
The wild colt's fillies.

Upon his wrist-bone
The robin settles;
While Chatzkel crams her
With lilac petals.

And then, in the Spring-time
Chatzkel sets free
Beast and bird under
The greenwood tree.

O, what was Nimrod
Who used strength, not skill,
To quell the forest,
Compared to Chatzkel,

Chatzkel who whistled
To catch a bird;
Who hallooed, and found him
In midst of a herd?

Scholar

A goat a scholar,
A goat a sage,
That ate *gemara*
From a grassy page!

Hot for wisdom
His dry mouth lipped
The small green mosses, —
His *rashi* script.

For higher lore
He chewed red clover;
He conned his Torah
Over and over.

And when his throat
Went dry on this book,
He ran and drank from
A garrulous brook.

Then up on his two
Hind legs stood he
And scratched his horns
Against a tree.

And crooned a *mishna*
In a voice most weird,
And nodded his wise pate,
And shook his beard.

Upon my word,
A learned one!
A scholar out of
Babylon!

Bestiary

God breathe a blessing on
His small bones, every one!
The little boy, who stalks
The Bible's plains and rocks
To hunt in grammar'd woods
Strange litters and wild broods;
The little boy who seeks
Beast-muzzles and bird-beaks
In cave and den and crypt,
In copse of holy script;
The little boy who looks
For quarry in holy books.

Before his eyes is born
The elusive unicorn;
There, scampering, arrive
The golden mice, the five;
Also in antic shape,
Gay peacock and glum ape.
He hears a snort of wrath:
The fiery behemoth!
And then on biblic breeze
The crocodile's sneeze . . .
He sees the lion eat
Green stalks . . . At tigress-teat
As if of the same ilk,
The young lamb sucking milk.

Hard by, as fleet as wind,
They pass, the roe and hind.
Bravely, and with no risk,
He halts the basilisk,
Pygarg and cockatrice.
And there, most forest-wise
Among the bestiaries,
The little hunter eyes
Him crawling at his leisure:
The beast Nebuchadnezzar.

I am weak before the wind; before the sun
    I faint; I lose my strength;
I am utterly vanquished by a star;
    I go to my knees, at length

Before the song of a bird; before
    The breath of spring or fall
I am lost; before these miracles
    I am nothing at all.

Orders

Muffle the wind;
Silence the clock;
Muzzle the mice;
Curb the small talk;
Cure the hinge-squeak;
Banish the thunder.
Let me sit silent,
Let me wonder.

About the Words

Aleph: the first letter of the Hebrew alphabet.

Basilisk: a mythical reptile, said to be hatched by a serpent from a cock's egg. Its poison was strong enough to break stones. Its look could kill.

Behemoth: a Biblical word for the largest and strongest of animals, probably the hippopotamus.

Bestiaries: many were written during the Middle Ages describing the habits of both real and mythical animals.

Burgher: the citizen of a town.

Cockatrice: a later name for the basilisk. It was often shown with the head and wings of a cock and the tail of a serpent.

Gemara: see *Talmud.*

Kosher: food or articles that have been prepared according to Jewish law.

Mishna: see *Talmud.*

Modeh Ani: the first words of a traditional Jewish prayer said on getting up in the morning, especially by children, meaning "I will give thanks."

Nebuchadnezzar: a wicked king of Babylon who is said to have ended his days as a grass-eating animal.

Nimrod: an early king of Assyria. He is mentioned in the book of Genesis: "the first on earth to be a mighty man . . . a mighty hunter before the Lord."

Pygarg: a kind of antelope described by several ancient authors, meaning "the white-rumped animal."

Rashi: Rashi (Rabbi Solomon ben Isaac) was a famous scholar who lived in France during the 11th Century. His commentary on the Bible was so clear that it is still used today.

Sambation: perhaps a real and certainly a legendary river. Some say that it ran only one day in seven, on the Sabbath. Others claim it ran for six days and rested on the Sabbath. It may have been the site of the exile of the Ten Tribes of Israel after the Assyrians destroyed their kingdom in 721 BC.

Shtreimel: a round fur-trimmed hat worn by the Chassidic Jews of Eastern Europe on the Sabbath and holidays.

Talmud: a collection of interpretations of the first five books of the Bible. The *Talmud* is made up of two parts: the *Mishna,* or moral laws, and the *Gemara,* which is a rabbinical commentary on the *Mishna.*

Tauph: the twenty-second and last letter of the Hebrew alphabet.

Torah: the first five books of the Bible, which includes the law of Moses and the whole of traditional Jewish wisdom, literature, and culture.

About the Author

"He was such fun to be with."
P.K. Page

Abraham Moses Klein (1909-1972) was born in Ratno, a small Russian Jewish town in the Ukraine. In 1910 his family moved to Canada where his gentle father found work as a clothes presser in the garment industry in Montreal.

Abraham Klein had a happy childhood in the beautiful old city where a large and lively Jewish community was sandwiched between English-speaking Protestants to the west and French-speaking Catholics to the east. He preferred books to sports. During his first swimming lesson, he almost drowned in four feet of water and had to be fished out with a pole! In high school his friends noticed him reading the dictionary from cover to cover as if it were a novel.

He received an excellent education, studying Arts at McGill University and Law at l'Université de Montréal. He grew up fluent in four languages — English, French, Hebrew, and Yiddish. A friend remembered: "you could tell he loved words just by the way he rolled them out. He didn't just toss off his good lines, he savored them."

Although he did not become a rabbi as some of his teachers hoped, Abraham Klein was steeped in family memories of Ratno and the traditions of his people. "They dwell in my veins, they eavesdrop at my ear,/They circle, as with Torahs, round my skull." It is this lost Eastern European world, soon to be destroyed by Hitler's Nazis, that is recreated in the poems Klein wrote for his nephews and nieces when he was a young man. They are a spirited mixture of nursery rhymes and Yiddish folk songs, "Chassidic dream kingdoms of Jewish lore." They are full of gaiety, jokes, and word games, inhabited by royal pedlars, learned goats, and dancing prophets.

Klein lived his adult life "like a personal five-ring circus." He wrote novels and plays and poetry; speeches for a whisky baron and for the Commonwealth Co-operative Federation's political party meetings. He ran for Parliament, unsuccessfully; worked as a lawyer, not very successfully; and as a journalist, editor, and university lecturer. But he always had time for family and friends.

The poems in this book appear in *A.M. Klein: Complete Poems* © University of Toronto Press 1990 and are reprinted here with the permission of the University of Toronto Press and the Estate of A.M. Klein.

Illustrations copyright © Gail Geltner, 1990.

The publisher thanks The Canada Council, the Ontario Arts Council, and the Department of the Secretary of State, Multiculturalism Sector, for assistance in publishing this book.

Canadian Cataloguing in Publication Data

Klein, A.M. (Abraham Moses), 1909-1972
Doctor Dwarf and other poems for children

ISBN 0-919627-41-2 (bound) -
ISBN 0-919627-43-9 (pbk.)

   1. Jews — Folklore — Juvenile poetry. 2. Legends, Jewish—Juvenile poetry. 3. Bible. O.T. — Legends — Juvenile poetry. I. Downie, Mary Alice, 1934- . II. Robertson, Barbara, 1931- . III. Geltner, Gail, 1944- . IV. Title.

PS8521.L45D63 1989 jC811'.54   c89-090310-7
PZ8.3.K44Do 1989

Design by Keith Abraham.

Printed and bound in Canada by Tri-Graphic Printing, Ottawa, Ontario.

Distributed in Canada by the University of Toronto Press, 5201 Dufferin Street, Downsview, Ontario M3H 5T8 and in The United States of America by Bookslinger, 502 North Prior Avenue, St. Paul, Minnesota 55104.

Published by Quarry Press, Inc., P.O. Box 1061, Kingston, Ontario K7L 4Y5 and P.O. Box 348, Clayton, New York 13624.